CLOSE THE BACK DOOR

SOLUTIONS FOR RETAINING RESIDENTS IN MULTIFAMILY COMMUNITIES

Elaine M. Simpson

OCCUPANCY
SOLUTIONS, LLC

CLOSE THE BACK DOOR: SOLUTIONS FOR RETAINING RESIDENTS IN MULTIFAMILY COMMUNITIES.

ISBN-13: 978-0-578-53670-5

Contact:
Elaine M. Simpson
Occupancy Solutions
esimpson@occupancysolutions.com
www.OccupancySolutions.com
(800) 865-0948

Cover design by Anamorphics, Inc.

CONTENTS

INTRODUCTION

P EOPLE LIKE TO LIVE where they feel like a part of a community. We used to say "properties", but now we call them communities, and for good reason. The first step in creating a community is for the onsite team to provide exceptional customer service to every resident, visitor, prospect, vendor, and co-worker. Things break, and mistakes happen. It is how you respond to those events that matters. Residents want and deserve to have you swiftly address and correct problems in the community. They want service with a smile, for you to listen with the intent to understand them, and to ask questions so you completely understand their concern. Residents want you to follow up with them to make sure they feel taken care of.

With today's market saturated with so many housing options, many communities are similar in age, amenities, finishes, layouts, and location. The biggest difference is the onsite team, a team that can retain more residents based on how we treat them and take care of them. Creating loyalty and increasing resident retention will, over time, reduce your expenses and maximize your income.

Using the methods in this book, you will also create better places to live, occupied by happier residents, with fewer problems and less crime, where people truly value and take pride in their community. I developed these methods during my 30 years as a property management professional, and I trust they will help you as much as they helped me and my residents.

For additional resources including the worksheets and documents mentioned throughout this book please visit **www.occupancysolutions.com/resources**.

Elaine M. Simpson
Occupancy Solutions

1

RESIDENTS BREAK LEASES OR DO NOT WANT TO RENEW

V ACANCY IS THE RESULT of too few move-ins and too many move-outs. This chapter offers five solutions to the move-outs. Some of them might seem counterintuitive, because they appear to reduce the number of potential residents who could move in. But in the long run, these solutions increase occupancy rates and reduce delinquencies and vacancies.

Solution 1:
Be more selective and increase your minimum income requirement.

In the multifamily industry, there is no rule on how high or low the minimum income requirement must be in a community. The industry standard is typically two to three times the monthly rent. You may want to consider a higher minimum income requirement if one of the following occurs:

- In most months, residents do not pay rent on time.
- Residents are being evicted due to nonpayment of rent.

An eviction can cost from $3,500 to $10,000 and can include legal fees and court costs, property damages, and lost rent. Not included in this amount is the cost of losing good residents due to this non-paying resident.

It doesn't matter if you have a conventional community or an affordable community, also known as an income-restricted community. Even an affordable community that has Low-Income Housing Tax Credits can have the minimum income set at a level that allows for selecting potential residents who will not be struggling paycheck-to-paycheck but who also meet the maximum income requirements determined by the low-income housing program.

When an owner or management agent is struggling with occupancy, they usually call in a consultant to help determine the best way to solve the problem. When my company, Occupancy Solutions, is engaged to analyze why a community has a vacancy problem, we look at the whole picture, from the resident selection criteria to why past residents moved out. We often recommend increasing the minimum income requirement to target residents who can afford to live more comfortably with the monthly rent commitment.

This suggestion is often met with hesitation because increasing the minimum income requirement decreases the number of potential residents who qualify to live in the community. But, while this solution might reduce the number of move-ins, it also reduces the number of move-outs!

The residents who qualify with the higher minimum income requirement are less likely to struggle each month to meet their rental obligation. When residents don't struggle each month financially, they are happier. And that makes your job easier.

Unhappy residents can make the management and maintenance staff miserable, and they can negatively affect other residents. People who live around or encounter the unhappy resident may decide to move out so that they can avoid interacting with that person. This increases vacancy and potentially causes a negative reputation for your community.

In the late 1990s, I managed one of the first Low-Income Housing Tax Credit communities in Michigan. Low-Income Housing Tax Credit (LIHTC) communities, also known as Workforce housing, are income-restricted and rent-restricted. In an income-restricted community, each household must be at or below the maximum income level for the program(s) at the community. The maximum income is determined by the Area Median Income (AMI) and is adjusted based on the total number of occupants in the household.

Due to the income restrictions at the LIHTC community in Michigan, the rent-to-income ratio was very high, and most—if not all—the residents were living paycheck to paycheck.

The community experienced a lot of resident turnover, and most of the move-outs were due to eviction or residents skipping (abandoning the premises) in the middle of the night to avoid eviction. The resident selection criteria required, in addition to the maximum income set by the program, a minimum income requirement set by the management agent. The minimum income was two times the monthly rent.

For example, for a two-bedroom renting for $750 per month, the minimum income for a household of four people was $1500 per month. If half the income was going towards rent, that left only $750 per month to pay for utilities, car payments, groceries, and childcare. That could leave the household struggling to pay rent most months, and it often resulted in either a skip, a lease break, or an eviction for non-payment.

To address the delinquency and vacancy problem, I analyzed those residents who had been evicted or broke their lease. All these previous residents had qualified with an income above two times the monthly rent, but below 2.5 times the monthly rent. The minimum income requirement was clearly too low and needed to be increased to three times the monthly rent.

It is not common practice, especially in the affordable multifamily industry, to increase the monthly income requirements. If you are program-related like we were, you are focused on not going over the maximum allowable income. Often the mindset is that we must accept anyone who meets our minimum and maximum income requirements.

This is true, but why not accept the best of the best? The programs only refer to the maximum income requirements, not the minimum income. The management agent or the owner of the property typically sets the minimum. With a higher minimum income requirement, residents will have a lower rent-to-income ratio and therefore have more money to pay rent each month.

I convinced the owner of the community to increase the minimum income requirement to 2.5 times the monthly rent. Initially, our closing ratio (the number of applications taken per the number of prospects through our front door) suffered a bit, and we did not have as many move-ins.

But after two months, we rebounded from 87% occupancy and achieved 96% occupancy. We gained a more financially stable resident population. Although we had fewer prospects who qualified, we got a better selection of residents who did not struggle every month to pay their rent. Delinquency decreased, and resident turnover decreased considerably. More residents lived out their leases and renewed for the next year.

Overall, our occupancy only suffered for a short time, and our economic occupancy increased to be much closer to our physical occupancy. (Economic occupancy is the amount of money collected from current renters, as opposed to the maximum amount that could be collected for a fully occupied property that offered no discounts.)

The Big Idea

Implementing a higher minimum income requirement creates a smaller pool of potential residents to choose from, but the people who qualify and move in are better and happier residents. Residents who don't struggle each month to pay their rent live out the term of the lease, increasing resident retention and reducing delinquency.

Solution 2:
Be more selective and increase the community's minimum credit requirement.

When a property struggles to retain residents, management often focuses on how to retain current residents without asking whether those residents should have been approved in the first place. Are your credit score requirements high enough to only qualify those who can afford to live in your community? If you accept low credit scores, you are setting your residents up to fail.

A low minimum credit requirement affects your community in two ways.

First, a lower credit score requirement allows people who may have a history of slow payments to be approved and move in. Management will need to spend more time working on reducing delinquency, taking residents to court, and possibly evicting the residents. Court costs are incurred in each step of the court process, and most courts now require the management agent to hire an attorney to file the paperwork and make the court appearances. This adds even more to the cost of an eviction. In most cases, the resident can be charged for these expenses; but if the resident is having trouble paying rent, they probably can't afford to pay the added expenses, and collection may be a challenge.

Second, in many cases, residents with poor credit tend to abuse their apartment, the apartment community, and amenities more than those with better credit. This results in damages to the apartment and community, and it causes neighboring residents to move out due to noise, traffic, infestations, and other related issues.

In my property management career, I worked at a variety of communities from low-income to luxurious high rises. One was a beautiful luxury community with more than 400 apartments, incredible amenities, and expansive green space with numerous ponds. At the time, there was no other community like it in our market. Many prospects wanted to live there. We didn't worry about the turnover, because we had so many interested, potential residents.

Although we consistently maintained an above-average

occupancy of 95–97%, many residents were not fulfilling their lease obligations and breaking their leases after just a few months. Why? These residents seemed to like living at our community. They referred their coworkers, friends, and family to us. It made no sense that they were leaving halfway through their leases. We asked residents why they were moving, and most of them gave various reasons or excuses. In most cases, the explanations were not related to financial challenges.

I reviewed these residents' rent payment histories, and most were consistently late. I reviewed each of the residents' files from cover to cover, including the conversation log in each file. Many of the logs documented conversations in which the residents expressed their frustration over their struggle to keep current on their monthly rent commitment. These same residents appeared to be unhappy and very disgruntled, and it got worse every time they received late notices, late fees, and notices for court appearances related to their nonpayment of rent. They just couldn't get ahead.

Next, I examined each of their applications, including credit reports, and noted in an Excel spreadsheet their credit scores compared to our minimum credit requirement of 630. Many of these lease-breaking residents had credit scores between 630 and 685. I then looked at the residents who had a good payment history with us, and their credit scores were all above 705. It appeared that our minimum credit requirement was too low, and it allowed people who could not afford to live at our community to move in.

If we increased the credit requirement to 700, the number of people who would qualify would be reduced, but we would also reduce the number of residents moving out due to financial struggles related to rent. We increased the credit requirement to 700 and, after a slight setback, we rebounded to 96% occupancy. The new residents who did not struggle to pay rent were a better clientele, and they referred and attracted others with similar credit scores. We found that our residents were better qualified, paid their rent on time, stayed with us longer, and referred others because they were happy.

The Big Idea

Select the best of the best by setting more stringent credit requirements—and don't make exceptions. A higher credit score requirement creates a smaller pool of potential residents to choose from, but the residents who qualify and move in are better, happier residents. They value their credit score and take better care of their home and the community, and they don't disturb their neighbors. As a result, residents and staff are happier.

Solution 3:
Make landlord reference checks a part of your resident screening process.

You find out a lot about prospective residents by checking landlord references. You can usually find out if the potential resident paid their rent on time, which is important because there is a lag time for evictions and judgments to appear on credit reports. You can also discover if the potential resident had any problems with other residents, damaged their home, complied with the lease and rules and regulations, and if they had an unusual number of guests or heavy traffic. Unfortunately, very few management companies and owners perform this crucial step in the due diligence process for selecting residents.

I was contacted by a potential client who owned a 100-unit property. He was struggling with delinquencies, high turnover, and low occupancy. During the operations portion of my assessment to determine his problems and potential solutions, the manager explained their application process to me. It was simple but incomplete. Mr. Resident would complete the application, and management would run the criminal background check. If the result was acceptable, the manager ran the credit report. If the credit was acceptable, the manager verified Mr. Resident's income and employment. If Mr. Resident's income met the requirements, the manager informed him that he was approved.

The one step the manager missed was the landlord reference.

Mr. Resident moved in and paid his rent on time each month, but the manager started to become concerned about the noise complaints from the neighbors who reported loud music and lots of guests that stayed only 10–20 minutes at a time. Mr. Resident was either a partier with no regard for his neighbors and lease obligations, or he was participating in an illegal activity such as dealing drugs.

A resident like this might stay for years at your community, because he isn't going anywhere as long as he can do whatever he wants. But the good, loyal residents surrounding him will move out due to noise, traffic, and the shady characters coming and going at all hours of the night.

By checking landlord references, you discover things about your potential residents that otherwise you would not experience until after they move in and cause physical damage or cause good residents to move out. With landlord reference checks, management finds out if potential residents paid their rent on time, had any problems with other residents, destroyed their apartment, complied with the lease and rules and regulations, and if they had an unusual number of guests.

The Big Idea

Requiring current and previous landlord reference checks empowers you to weed out and deny the potential residents with poor payment histories and lease violations, and those who would possibly drive out their future neighbors. Residents selected using income, credit, and landlord reference checks are better, happier residents who will stay longer. Their neighbors will also be happier residents who stay longer.

Solution 4:
Schedule time with new residents before the move-in date to review their leases and all the obligations.

Ignorance is not bliss. I'm sure you've heard the following statements from a resident: "I didn't know," or "I don't remember reading that in the lease," or, my favorite, "That was not in the lease I signed." How many times do you hear these responses from residents who violated the lease or didn't understand what they agreed to?

It is our job as property management professionals to do everything we can to make sure our residents read and understand their lease obligations. This is crucial to having happy, long-term residents. When you educate your new residents, you increase resident retention because your residents are aware of the lease terms, policies, rules and regulations, and the consequences if the rules are not followed. This leaves no room for surprises.

To focus the resident on the lease, have them come in a couple of days before their move-in date, and let them know that the lease review and signing will take approximately an hour. (It might take longer or shorter depending on your property.) This gives the resident a chance to focus instead of rushing through the lease because they are eager to move into their new apartment and start unpacking.

You've probably met Mr. Resident who arrives to sign his lease, pay his rent, receive his keys, and move in, maybe with friends and family waiting in the parking lot ready to help. Maybe you did not go through the lease with Mr. Resident to explain and educate him on what the landlord/resident relationship is all about. Maybe there was no discussion about what was expected of Mr. Resident, or the penalties if he did not comply with the lease and the rules. Maybe you assumed he wouldn't sign a contract unless he understood everything about it. Maybe you were just busy.

But residents who do not review the lease thoroughly often become problem residents who always respond to notices of lease violations with an irate "I didn't know," or "I don't remember agreeing to this." Meanwhile, their neighbors are moving out because they don't want to put up with those residents' lease violations.

My solution to this problem is to schedule the lease

signing at least a day before the move-in date and inform Mr. Resident that he and I will review the lease, and that I will answer all his questions before he signs on the dotted line. I tell him to plan on about an hour for this meeting.

This meeting gives Mr. Resident a chance to be relaxed, calm, and focused—not rushing through the lease, but taking his time to fully understand the legal contract he is signing. He can review the lease and other policies and discuss with me at length about what he is agreeing to and what is expected of him. When he is ready to sign, Mr. Resident completely understands his obligations and what to expect from our relationship.

The Big Idea

A one-hour lease-review meeting before the move-in date results in residents who fulfill their leases happily and loyally because they have no misconceptions about what is expected of them and what management will and will not tolerate. Communication and education are crucial to establishing a good business relationship between management and residents.

Solution 5:
Educating potential residents about communal living will improve their experience at your community.

Apartment life is different than living without people above, below, or next to you. Sounds travel, smells travel, and residents will be living with people who are not family or friends, and whom they might not like.

I once worked at a 55-and-older community that was attracting many seniors who were moving from a single-family home and had not lived in an apartment in a very long time or may have never lived in an apartment. This was evident when I moved Ms. Smith into her new apartment. She was selling her home and had not lived in a communal situation since her college dorm days. Shortly after she moved in, she started complaining of a strange odor coming from the apartment next door. The odor was in the building hallway and seeping into her apartment through a vent in her second bedroom. The odor was strong and did not seem to be going away. Ms. Smith also started complaining about how the hard-walking resident above her was making it difficult to enjoy her apartment.

The smell was curry, and the person above her was a fairly large man. Ms. Smith decided she could not live like that, and she moved out in the middle of the night.

I assumed Ms. Smith did not like communal living and was better off living somewhere else. My supervisor felt differently and said that if I had spent more time educating Ms. Smith on what to expect, then she would have been better prepared and more understanding.

I thought about this and realized my job was not just

getting people to move in but to educate them on what to expect so they would be happier residents. I committed to not just selling the benefits of living at my community but to educating prospects about communal living during the tour and especially during the lease signing. I prepared my prospects on what to expect, so they had an opportunity to decide whether communal living was right for them.

During the interviews and tours of my community, I would find out if prospects had ever lived in an apartment and if so, how long ago. I asked what their experience was like. If it was positive, great! If not, then I had an opportunity to remind them of what they disliked about communal living, and suggest they consider another type of housing. If they had never lived in a community like mine, I took the time to review what life is like and what to expect with neighbors above, below, next door, and down the hall.

Remember that this discussion must be kept general. Never disclose any information about your residents, and never violate fair housing laws.

Although this process may lose a potential resident, those who do move in will be much happier in the long run—and so will you.

The Big Idea

Helping residents understand what to expect from communal living will either prepare them properly or help them realize that apartment living is not for them.

2

RESIDENTS DON'T SEE THE VALUE OF THE COMMUNITY

Y OUR RESIDENTS NEED to experience and understand the value you offer them. Once your residents understand the value, they become loyal, stay longer, and refer potential residents.

Solution 1:
Demonstrate value by proactively contacting residents to see what maintenance needs to be done on their apartment, or if they have any other concerns.

Renters want to be taken care of. By some estimates, 43% of renters value maintenance-free living. In other words, almost half of your residents choose to be renters so they can enjoy maintenance-free living. Being proactive about maintenance is a great way to demonstrate the value you bring to their lives.

I remember a young, newly married couple who moved into their first apartment after both living at their parents' homes. During the tour, the two of them held hands, giggling and whispering to each other. Excitement and eagerness were in the air. I showed them around the community: the fitness center, the business center, the outdoor swimming pool, and the apartment that I had determined met their needs based on the information they had shared with me.

Within seconds of entering the vacant apartment, the newlyweds were imagining hosting holiday dinners and parties in their new home. They planned on making the second bedroom an office or possibly a guest room until they were ready to have their first child, which they figured would be a few years down the road. They eagerly paid the deposit and quickly provided all the information they needed to be approved. The couple moved into their new home two weeks later.

Things seemed to be going great. The couple made no complaints and never put in any service requests. They always paid their rent on time. They were the perfect residents! I assumed they loved their first home. Nine months into their lease, I sent them a renewal notice stating that their lease would end in three months and that we'd like them to renew for another year.

Suddenly, they informed me of several problems with their apartment, inconveniences such as a dripping faucet, an outlet that wasn't working, a hole in the screen door to their patio, and upstairs neighbors who walked loudly. It wasn't until they got the renewal notice that they started to consider the past nine months. The questioned whether they were truly happy and if the rent was really worth it for a place they felt was not terrible but not that great either. They searched other housing options and decided to move at the end of their lease.

What went wrong? Did I fail the newlyweds because I did

not check on them and ask how they liked living at the community? Could I have retained them if I had regularly asked what needed to be corrected in their home or what concerns they might have had?

It comes down to this: they didn't feel that the value they received was worth their rent, and I never found out that they felt this way because I never checked on them to ask.

As a result, I changed how we showed value to our residents. I made a conscious effort to maintain relationships with our residents, check in with them, and show them value by the way we cared for them. The whole site team was included in this, and we were determined to change and prove our value to our prospects and residents. We developed a plan in which everyone had an important role. We worked on determining what our residents found valuable.

A couple weeks later, a young man was looking to move in from out of town. He was being transferred within his company to our area. I showed him all the amenities and the apartment, and I noted all his comments. He loved the apartment, and I wanted to be sure he understood the value. We reviewed the lease and discussed living at our community, what the community offered, and how and when he should let us know when something needed attention in his apartment.

We then went to his apartment, and I showed him where the circuit breaker box was located and how to flip the breaker if an outlet or switch didn't work. I showed him where the garbage-disposal crank was and how to use it if the disposal stopped working. I explained the heating/cooling system and that the light switch in the bedroom controlled the outlet on the wall.

Every time the young man paid his rent, regardless of

who took the payment, he was asked what needed to be corrected in his apartment and how he liked living with us. If something needed to be fixed, we opened a service request right then. We were also careful to ask, "*What* needs to be addressed in the apartment?" This is an open-ended question, and it is better than a close-ended question such as, "Do you have anything that needs to be addressed in the apartment?" Asking the open-ended question prompted the resident to think differently and come up with things he was concerned about.

At least once a month, a staff member would call him or leave a note on his door to say "hi", ask if he needed anything addressed in his home, and tell him that we wanted to make sure he was happy with everything. We sent him a birthday card. We sent thank-you cards whenever he notified us of anything that needed fixing in his apartment or in the community.

In the same month he moved in, we started hosting monthly happy hours for the residents, and we introduced him to other residents, helping him feel like a part of the community. We did preventative maintenance inspections and corrected things immediately. We worked hard to maintain the community and keep it clean.

The young man renewed the first year and stayed with us for six years. He referred four new residents to us. When he moved out, I pulled him aside to thank him and to ask him what he liked most about living with us. His response nearly brought tears to my eyes.

He said that when he moved in from another state, not really knowing anyone in the city, the efforts we made to connect him with other residents and regularly check on him made him feel like he was a part of our family. He said we took wonderful care of him. He liked me and my team because we were friendly, polite, professional, and took care of things immediately. He said he was dreading leaving, because he really wanted to stay with us!

The Big Idea

Checking on your residents to make sure everything is okay makes them feel cared for, increases their loyalty, and brings you new referral business.

Solution 2:
Know who your residents are comparing you to, so you can compete better.

It is much easier to compete when you know who you are competing against, what you have that is better than your competition, and what the competitor has that is better than your community. This tells you what you need to overcome.

You know what happens when we assume, right? I assumed something with residents many years ago, and I learned a big lesson! I was managing a community where many good residents were moving out—the kind of residents we loved and didn't want to lose. What was happening?

I reviewed the previous residents' files to see where they were moving. I had assumed they were all buying homes, because why else would they leave us? To my surprise, they were moving into our competition and some communities I had never heard of before. Why would they move there?

Why didn't they like us anymore? What did these communities have that made them more attractive?

I had been so wrapped up in what we offered at my community that I never bothered to check out what the competition offered. This was a big mistake, and I should have known better! I had grown up as a competitive swimmer, and my coach prepared us for swim meets by analyzing our strengths and weaknesses compared to the opposing team. Since a swimmer could only swim in so many events at a given meet, the coach used his analysis to choose which events each swimmer would enter based on the entire team's needs compared to the competition to win the swim meet.

I needed to do the same with my community. How could I compete when I didn't know who or what I was competing against? I immediately pulled out our market comparison spreadsheet, which hadn't been updated in several months. I compared the list of competitors on the spreadsheet with the communities I was losing residents to. To my surprise, several communities taking my residents were not in my market comparison. I had a lot of work to do!

I discovered my residents were moving to communities that had a dog run, a 24-hour fitness center, and a "satisfaction guarantee" that if a resident was not happy for any reason, the resident could be released from the lease with only a 30-day written notice.

These were the reason my residents moved out? I wish I had known sooner, because I could offer these to my residents, too!

Since many residents see their dogs as their children, I didn't just add a dog *run*—I installed a dog *park*! As a result, dogs and their owners wanted to live at my community more than a community with just a dog run. I had a beautiful fitness center, but it was only open during business hours, which didn't work for most residents who wanted to work out before or after work. So, I installed a card reader and put a camera in the fitness center. It didn't cost much, and the cost would easily be justified if I could save one or two residents. The satisfaction guarantee was a little more difficult, because it was an unknown. But if we focused on adding value, the residents wouldn't feel like moving.

Now we check on what our competition is doing on an ongoing basis. We informally check in with current residents when collecting rent or writing service requests. We communicate through surveys and interviews to make sure we know our residents' concerns and desires. With so much competition out there, we need to make sure that our residents are getting value—or they will go somewhere else.

The Big Idea

If you don't provide for your residents, the competition will. Find out what your competition is offering and communicate with your residents to find out what they value in a community. Then you can meet their needs and keep them as loyal residents.

Solution 3:
Partner with others, so you can
better compete and add value.

In May 2017, the National Apartment Association published

the results of a nationwide study which included 43 unique amenities that were added or upgraded from January 2014 to September 2016. The survey analyzed 100,000 responses in 35 states.

Five of the top 10 amenities added or upgraded since 2014 involve bringing people together—the community aspect of apartment living that is a draw to so many residents. Clubhouses and common areas for socializing made the top five, with swimming pools, outdoor kitchens, and play areas also proving popular.

How can you compete against other communities that have larger budgets and better amenities when you only have so much space and limited funds? How do you add value when you can't build anything or afford to bring services in? How do you add an amenity when you don't have the space or the resources to add a swimming pool, a clubhouse with space for private parties, a business center, or a fitness room?

The answer: you get creative and look for ways to partner with other businesses to better compete in your market.

I have worked at many communities that had few to no amenities, and communities where, due to their age, the amenities were outdated and, as a result, the communities had difficulty competing in their market. One community had been built in the 1970s and completely lacked amenities. This community was competing with a brand-new one next door that had a beautiful fitness center, swimming pool, business center, and community room.

What could I do to add these amenities to my community so my residents and prospective residents would get the value they desired and want to live at my community? After many hours of soul searching, I realized I could not do it on my own. I needed partners to provide those amenities.

I created a chart with four columns: Fitness Center, Swimming Pool, Business Center, and Community Room. Below each column title, I listed businesses in the area that had that particular amenity. If I couldn't think of any businesses, I searched for them on the Internet. Soon I had several businesses that I planned to contact in hopes of creating a partnership so I could stay competitive.

After many telephone calls and meetings, I was able to provide those amenities to my residents and potential residents. For a fitness option, I worked with a small, independent gym within walking distance of my community. We agreed to allow the gym to put advertisements in our move-in packets. In exchange, the gym waived the initial membership fee and offered a significant reduction in the monthly membership fee.

The swimming pool was a bit more challenging, but I worked out a deal with a small motel within a mile of the community where my residents could use the motel's pool for $2.00 per person per day. This was in Michigan, and it was not a tourist area, so the motel suffered with low occupancy during the summer months. The motel appreciated the additional income, while my residents enjoyed cooling off in the motel's pool on a hot and humid summer day.

For the business center, I connected with the local library that had computers. I encouraged my residents to get library cards, which benefited the library and resulted in Internet and computer access for my residents. Another option is to partner with a community center or a business service center such as a FedEx or UPS office center.

Across the street from my community was a VFW hall, and I worked out a deal to allow the hall to put flyers in my move-in packets in exchange for a discount to my residents to host events at the venue. Plus, I hosted resident events in the hall, which encouraged more rentals by our residents when they got to see first-hand how nice the hall was.

Most of my residents were thrilled. Some would have preferred to have the amenity onsite at the community or included in the rent, but many appreciated it. Some admitted that the selling benefit of the amenity was important, but after they moved in, they realized they didn't use the amenity as much as they had anticipated, if at all. Think of that treadmill you have in your basement—the one currently being used for a clothes rack.

You need to constantly check on the competition and figure out ways to compete against the latest and greatest amenity they've added. Then, figure out how to provide that amenity for your residents, and follow up by letting your residents know that you did it for them, and what the value is.

The Big Idea

Don't be defeated by an apparent lack of time or resources. Look for other options and brainstorm solutions for business partnerships so you can add value for your residents and compete against those communities that have many amenities.

Solution 4:
To find out what residents value, ask them!

Over the years, I got the impression that my residents thought I was a mind reader because they would move out and never tell me that they didn't like something or that I was lacking a desired a service or amenity. Every Monday, I looked at my reports which showed the previous week's activity, including traffic, leases, notices to vacate, move-ins, and move-outs. Each week, I sent my properties questions about the reports. When I asked why someone had moved out or given a notice of intent to move out, I would get vague answers that amounted to "We don't know."

Why were we losing our residents? What could we do to save them?

Whenever an employee left my company, she would be asked to complete an exit interview. We wanted to know what the employee thought about their time at our company—the good, the bad, and the ugly. Why wasn't I doing the same practice with my residents? If I didn't know what was wrong or what they found to be of value, how could I improve my residents' experiences?

I implemented a new policy that when a resident moved out, an exit interview survey would be sent to them to better understand their experience with us. We started sending the same sort of survey to residents who gave us notice of their intent to move out. Maybe we could retain them if we understood what was important and valuable to them.

A few months later, we started to regularly check on current residents to see if we needed to redirect our energies to focus on providing value and meeting their needs and wants.

As an example, a current resident responded that it was difficult to have maintenance work done in his home because he needed to be there due to his dog, but he couldn't take time off from work to do it. This prompted me to reconsider how and when we provided service repairs for residents. I implemented a policy to provide scheduled maintenance repairs every other Saturday to accommodate residents' busy schedules.

By asking what residents want and value, we can modify policies and practices to accommodate them. This shows that we value their opinion, and it builds loyalty and retains residents.

The survey could be done online using Surveymonkey.com or your community's Facebook page, or it could be sent via email, or mailed as a paper survey.

TIPS FOR SURVEYS

- Keep survey short and sweet (five questions).

- Use rating systems that are easy for residents to interpret.

- Include a deadline for completing the survey.

- Include space for residents to add comments.

- Offer incentives to complete the survey, such as entering all completed surveys in a drawing for a $50 gift card or rent discount.

SUGGESTED SURVEY QUESTIONS

- What in your apartment or building needs to be repaired or addressed?

- What was your main reason for selecting our community?

- What services or social activities would you like to see offered here?

- How would you prefer we keep in touch with you?

- Would you refer someone to this community?

- Will you be staying with us when your lease is up for renewal?

EXAMPLE LETTER TO ACCOMPANY PAPER SURVEYS

Dear (Resident),

At (Management Company), we pride ourselves on listening and responding to our residents! You have been at (Community Name) a short time, but we would like to know how you feel about living in our community. We believe we are only as good as our residents feel we are doing!

So we can provide you with extraordinary customer service, we ask you to complete this very short survey anonymously. When you are done, please send it back to our corporate office using the enclosed self-addressed stamped envelope. Please do not deliver this survey to the office located at the community.

Any additional comments you would like to share below are greatly appreciated:

_____
_____
_____
_____
_____
_____

Sincerely,

(Name)
(Position)
(Community or Management Company)

EXAMPLE EMAIL FOR ONLINE SURVEY

Dear (Resident),

At (Management Company), we pride ourselves on listening and responding to our residents! You have been at (Community Name) a short time, but we would like to know how you feel about living in our community. We believe we are only as good as our residents feel we are doing!

So we can provide you with extraordinary customer service, we ask you follow this link to anonymously complete a very short online survey: (Hyperlink to Survey)

Sincerely,

(Name)
(Position)
(Community or Management Company)

The Big Idea

Ask your residents what they want and value. Use paper surveys, online surveys, or a suggestion box. Act on the responses.

Solution 5:
Compare the monthly cost of living at your community to the competition, or to owning a house.

Whether your residents are considering moving into another community or buying a house, you will be competing against their other housing options. Comparing the monthly cost of those options to the cost of living in your community is, in either case, the solution.

Sometimes it comes down to dollars and cents. Has a resident ever said to you, "I'm going to buy a house, because I am tired of wasting money renting an apartment."? How do you overcome that? Home ownership is the American Dream, right?

To combat this challenge, I use a comparison chart to show those residents what home ownership really costs, and I share it with residents who are considering leaving to buy a home.

In the following chart, the utility expenses are based on the HUD Utility Schedule Model (HUSM), which is updated annually. HUD posts this information online for anyone to use, including an online calculator, a calculator in Excel, and instructions:

https://www.huduser.gov/portal/resources/utilallo wance.html

A more thorough explanation of the HUSM is freely available online in the HUD Utility Allowance Guidebook:

https://www.hudexchange.info/resource/2267/utilit y-allowance-guidebook/

Alternately, you could use the estimated value of the included utilities for your apartment to explain to the resident the true cost of living in a house on a monthly basis.

Whenever you are competing with homeownership—even when potential residents are considering buying or staying in a house instead of renting at your community—use a comparison chart to help the resident truly understand the cost of living in a house compared to renting your apartment. You will find that often the resident has not considered all the real expenses of living in a home, and they will gain a new understanding of the value of renting your apartment.

You will find a cost comparison worksheet at **www.occupancysolutions.com/resources**.

AN EXAMPLE COST COMPARISON

Amenities and Services	Exceptional Living Apartments		Home Ownership	
Mortgage or Rent	$800		1020	*Based on House*
Property Taxes	0		130	*Based on Mortgage*
Property Insurance	35	*Renter's Insurance.*	100	*Based on Plan*
Transportation (senior community w Bus)	*N/A*		*N/A*	

Heat Expense	0	*included*	90 *Based on Est. Utility Allowance*
Electric Expense	40	*Based on Est. Utility Allowance*	75 *Based on Est. Utility Allowance*
Sewer & Water Expense	0	*included*	45 *Based on Est. Utility Allowance*
Trash Removal Expense	0	*included*	25 *Based on Est. Utility Allowance*
Lawn Maintenance Expense	0		150 *Averaged over 12 months*
Snow Removal Expense	0		100 *Averaged over 12 months*
Home Maintenance Repairs	0		100 *Averaged over 12 months*
Emergency Call Services	0		75 *Averaged over 12 months*
Other			
TOTAL MONTHLY COST:	**$875**		**$1910**

Home maintenance and repairs are more than expensive; they are time-consuming and inconvenient. Consider reminding the resident that once they own their own home, they will need to take care of everything that breaks, from a leaky faucet to a leaky roof. That means finding contractors, calling them and scheduling time with them, reviewing their work, and dealing with any unsatisfactory situations that might arise with them. Does your resident really want to deal with all that? Or would it be easier and less of a hassle to simply call your office and open a service request, and let you deal with all that?

Finally, security is a cost that potential homeowners don't always consider. With community living, people are always around, and a team is onsite to keep an eye on things. This brings a certain level of security, especially for single people or those who often travel. If your resident moves into a home, who will be there to look out for suspicious activity when they are away? Or even when they are home? Home security systems are available, but they become an added cost for homeowners. Is it a cost your residents have considered?

The Big Idea

Many renters do not recognize the financial value you provide and may consider moving into your competition or a house. If you can break down the costs for them, you can help them understand how they save money by living at your community.

3

RESIDENTS OBJECT TO RENT INCREASES

Solution 1:
Show the market rate compared to
the renewal rate.

It costs approximately five times more to replace a resident than it does to keep one. Replacement costs include vacancy, maintenance and replacement of items in an apartment, marketing and leasing efforts, as well as labor costs for office and maintenance staff and vendors.

At **www.occupancysolutions.com/resources** you will find a spreadsheet to help you calculate how much it costs to replace one of your residents, based on your community's expenses.

In most cases, current residents are paying less than the market rate, and you might think you need to get them up to current market rates. But they have been good and loyal residents. If you give them a "loyalty" discount, you will keep them, and you won't need to spend so much to replace them.

I sent a renewal notice to Mr. John, a resident at my community for three years. I wanted him to stay with us another year. I said his rent would be increased from $920 to $1104, which was the current market rate for his apartment. Mr. John was not happy with this 20% rent increase after being a good resident for years. He was outraged about being punished. He threatened to move out.

At first, I felt he was being a bit harsh. After all, a management company is a business that must do things to compete in the market and make money for the owners. But after I thought about it, Mr. John had a point. Remember, it costs approximately five times more to replace a resident than it does to keep one. Mr. John's current rent was $920 per month, which meant it would cost me about $4,600 to re-rent his apartment—not including the emotional cost of negative feelings, and the business repercussions of negative reviews.

The increase to bring that apartment up to the market rate would mean an additional $12,208 per year rent revenue. But I would not gain that much, probably only about $7600, because I would also spend approximately $4,600 to replace Mr. John. What could I do to make him happy and show that I valued him as a resident?

I sat down with Mr. John to present an offer to him. Before I started talking numbers, I explained to Mr. John that we valued him as a long-term resident and would like to have him stay with us. But I also explained that the cost of running the community had increased and unfortunately that affects the residents. I also shared the most recent market comparison, and I pointed out where his rent was in comparison to the market. Mr. John's new rent would still be considerably lower than other rents for a similar apartment in the market.

Mr. John was a successful businessman who understood the logical approach I was taking with him. He considered this information and said that although he understood all of it, his loyalty should mean something. He asked if I was willing to take the risk on replacing him with a new resident if he moved out.

I agreed those were good points. I suggested that instead of the 20% increase to bring him up to market, we would honor his loyalty by only increasing him 10%, and by giving him a 10% loyalty discount below the market rent.

After a bit of consideration, Mr. John agreed to this smaller increase and renewed.

This initiated a change in how we viewed our current residents and their rent compared to the market. We initiated a renewal policy that the maximum increase would be no more than 10%, and if an apartment was renting for less than 10% below the market rent, we would only increase it by 5%. We made the residents aware of the market rate compared to their renewal rate by including this information in their initial renewal letter. That letter also said that because of the resident's loyalty and exceptional history, they would receive a loyalty discount off the current market rent. This meant that we had a variety of rental rates at any one time, but that is easily tracked with software.

The Big Idea

Residents are less likely to move out if you review the current market rates and compare them to the increased rent amount offered with the lease renewal. Offering an increase that is still a substantial discount off current market rates makes residents feel appreciated. If they stay, then you have eliminated your expenses and labor to re-rent that apartment.

Solution 2:
Incentivize residents by rewarding them with a lower rent increase if they renew early instead of waiting.

Get a commitment from your residents early in the renewal process by offering progressive deadlines for specific rates. The sooner they, renew the lower the increase. This creates a sense of urgency, and residents feel they are getting a better deal. It also gives you a better idea of who will not be renewing, so you can prepare to replace them.

In the early 1990s, I would send out renewal notices about 45 days prior to the end of the lease. If, for example, a lease ended on July 31, a notice went out to the resident on or around June 15th. Some companies sent notices 60 or 90 days prior to the expiration due to a program requirement or because of their policy, but residents still had plenty of time to renew their leases or gave a notice to vacate at least 30 days prior to moving out.

The problem was that many times the residents would get their renewal letters and begin looking for another apartment, and we would not know until it was too late. By then, the residents were already going through the approval process with another apartment community and had even paid their deposit. So, when residents paid their final month's rent, they would include the notice to vacate. We could not save them.

That meant we were losing those residents and needed to re-rent their apartments based on their move-out dates. The average apartment community has about a 50% turnover rate per year. For my 400-unit community, that meant an average of almost 17 move-outs each month. This

put us in a mad rush to try to find renters who wanted those apartments soon after they were vacated—otherwise, we would lose a lot of income.

In response to the crazy scramble we had each month, we changed our process to encourage residents to renew early, and to give us a better idea of how many notices to vacate we might expect. We started sending out the renewal notices 90–120 days before the leases expired, with progressive renewal deadlines offering different new rent rates. The lowest increase coincided with the earliest deadline, the second lowest increase with the second deadline, and the highest rent increase with the latest renewal date.

If the lease expired on July 31, for example, we sent out the first renewal letter 120 days earlier on April 1. Using an example rent of $910 per month and a current market rent of $1100, the three options looked like this:

Renew by:	New Rent will be:
May 1	$955/month (5% increase, 13% below market rent)
June 1	$982/month (8% increase, 11% below market rent)
July 1	$1001/month (10% increase, 9% below market rent)

30 days later, we sent another notice with the remaining options. After another 30 days, we sent a notice with the last renewal option and included a month-to-month option.

The lease dates didn't change, just the commitment levels and deadline dates. We got leases signed even though the renewal dates were 60–90 days away. We also found that residents would give more than a 30-day notice, so we could re-rent their apartments quicker and minimize the vacancy loss. It was a win/win.

If you have a program attached to your community, it might limit your timeline, so know and stay within your program requirements.

The Big Idea

Use progressive deadlines and tiered renewal rates to incentivize residents to renew early and not look elsewhere.

Solution 3:
Offering a longer lease term allows residents to lock their current rates for longer, which reduces their stress over the potential rent increase every 12 months, and it makes them more likely to commit to a current increase and still be happy.

By signing a longer lease, a resident feels she is getting a bargain, because she doesn't need to deal with negotiating or renewing for 18 or 24 months or longer. This decreases resident turnover and leads to happier residents paying higher rent.

Early in my career, I assumed that a lease was always 12 months long. Sometimes, I might have done a six-month lease or a month-to-month lease if someone was anticipating a job transfer or if they were hoping to buy a house. But that was about it. A lease lasts a year.

Then a resident told me, "I feel like I just signed that 12-month lease yesterday. I can't believe it's time to sign *another* one." She was right. That year flies by, and each time we ask for a renewal, we risk that the resident might decide to move out.

What if I offered her an 18, 24, or 36-month lease? It would reduce my risk of losing her at the end of her lease. But would it make *her* feel better?

You might be thinking, "But a longer lease means you also lose out on a rent increase. What if the market goes crazy? What if you miss out on that higher potential rent?" Those are genuine concerns, and I came up with a solution that worked for both me and my resident. I looked at the market rent growth in our area. It was going up about 3% per year. So, I modified a three-year lease to say that I could increase rent up to 3% each year of the lease.

She loved this idea! She was eager to sign the lease and not need to worry about anything related to renewing her lease for the next 36 months. I felt great because I had one less lease renewal to worry about for the next three years, and my resident felt like I did her a favor.

I now offer a range of leases for renewal: 6, 12, 18, 24 and 36-month terms. The longer leases have rent increases built into them. My residents love the options, and they can choose the best option for them based on their current situation.

The Big Idea

Resident retention increases when you customize the length of your leases to meet residents' needs and desires.

Solution 4:
As an incentive for residents to renew their leases, provide a service that maintains or improves their apartment.

Residents value the service of adding an amenity or improvement. They feel they are getting something in return for their renewal. Even small improvements encourage residents to maintain their apartments in better condition. They see that you take pride in the community, and they take pride in it, too.

For years, I just sent out renewal letters to my residents and stated what the rent increase was and the deadline to sign their new leases. If residents did not renew, their leases would automatically convert to month-to-month leases. The lease renewal was all about the property, not about the resident. It was the one-sided *me, me, me* attitude of the letters which made residents feel like they weren't getting a fair shake.

This became increasingly evident when my retention numbers started to drop. I spoke with a few residents and discovered they felt like they were unimportant and not valued, because I didn't really give them anything.

I thought, "What can I do that would make it more of an exchange between us?" I came up with the renewal incentive plan in which I added value to the apartment instead of discounting rent. I created the "Anniversary Menu" which was available to residents who renewed for at least 12 months.

The Anniversary Menu is like celebrating a wedding anniversary, a time when people give gifts and plan a nice meal or a date at a fancy restaurant. Offering a menu of valuable services or amenities to the lease-renewal process gives residents the opportunity to choose what they would like in their apartment—a renewal gift. When residents can choose a gift from the menu, they feel like the process is an exchange and a happy celebration.

The first time I tested this process, it was a great success! Now it is standard practice to include the Anniversary Menu on my renewal notices. The service also helps an apartment keep its value because of preventative maintenance. For example, cleaning the carpet regularly helps the carpet last longer. It might not even need to be replaced when a resident moves out. Installing a ceiling fan where the bedroom overhead light used to be will add comfort and value for the current resident, but it is also and upgrade that increases the apartment's marketability.

Options for Your Anniversary Menu

- Clean the carpets.
- Install a ceiling fan.
- Upgrade the light fixtures.
- Deep clean the grout in bathrooms.
- Replace the blinds.
- Upgrade the plumbing fixtures (faucets and shower heads).
- Make the shower head adjustable.
- Upgrade the knobs and handles on cabinets and drawers.
- Paint an accent wall or two.
- Replace the light switch covers.
- Replace the toilet seat.

- Convert the thermostats to be programmable.
- Add shelves in a closet, if space allows.
- Refinish the bathtubs.
- Seal the countertops in the kitchen.
- Cut out a damaged area of a countertop and replace it with a cutting block.

The Big Idea

A resident who feels valued is more likely to renew a lease. Treat the renewal like an anniversary, and include, as a gift, improvements or upgrades to the resident's apartment.

4

RESIDENTS FEEL LIKE YOU ONLY FOCUS ON NEW RESIDENTS

Solution 1:
Create a Resident Retention Plan that communicates with the resident every month, from before the move-in through the end of the lease, instead of waiting until renewal time.

Typical management companies and communities use a marketing plan that focuses on bringing new prospective residents to the community to view apartments, following up with those prospects, and getting them to sign leases. But once the prospects become residents, no one checks on them. They only hear from the office when they have either done something wrong or the office needs something from them. Nine to eleven months later, residents get notices asking for another 12-month commitment. Often, the residents do not renew because they don't feel valued and don't have any loyalty to the staff or community.

My mother is a retired teacher who always said, "When students behave badly, we learn their names and get to know their parents quickly. But with well-behaved, good students, we don't learn their names and often never meet their parents." I feel the same way about residents. The ones who bring concerns to us or are problem residents, we get to know because we are in contact with them on a regular basis. But the good ones, the ones who are happy, pay their rent on time, don't violate their leases, or rarely contact us, we don't communicate with regularly, so we don't get to know them.

It costs approximately five times as much to re-rent an apartment home as it does to keep an existing resident. Multiply the cost of finding a new resident by the number of apartments in your community, then multiply that result by the national average of 50% for resident turnover. This will give you a ballpark figure of what vacancies are costing your community annually.

At **www.occupancysolutions.com/resources** you will find a worksheet to help you calculate these costs.

Create a Resident Retention Plan that provides many opportunities to connect with your residents. It will start with their move-in and continue all the way through the end of their lease, and it gets repeated every year. You will find a blank form to download at:

www.occupancysolutions.com/resources.

SEVEN STEPS TO CREATE A RESIDENT RETENTION PLAN

1. **Develop a Plan.** Make a timeline of scheduled communications to your residents.

2. **Implement the Plan**. Create the letters and purchase supplies.

3. **Follow Through.** Planning is the easy part, but your

follow through is the most important part. For a personal touch, always address the resident by name. Use the same letters and timing for every resident so you comply with fair housing regulations.

4. Use Questionnaires. Keep questionnaires short and simple. Incentivize residents to complete them by entering every completed questionnaire in a raffle. At the end of each quarter, randomly draw a winner who will receive a gift card.
5. Send Greeting Cards. Send handwritten cards personally addressed to each resident.

6. Incentivize Referrals. Throughout the year, offer a Resident Referral Reward and make all residents and their families aware of it.

7. Show Your Appreciation. Once a quarter or every other quarter, have a Resident Referral Drive, and at least once a year have a Resident Appreciation Week, or have a quarterly Resident Appreciation Day.

12-MONTH RESIDENT RETENTION MARKETING ACTION PLAN

Since each management company uses different titles, this plan uses "Community Coordinator" as a generic term for the person responsible for the task.

Time Frame	Retention Strategy	Suggested Action
Prior To Move-In	New Resident Orientation	Review the lease including all addenda and resident policies. Answer all the resident's questions.
Move-In Day	Staff Member escorts resident to new home and shows amenities.	Explain and demonstrate the features of the new home and community amenities. Offer a Move-In Gift.
7 Days After Move-In	Community Coordinator: Move-In Checklist and Move-In Questionnaire	Community Coordinator completes requests on Move-In Checklist and reviews Move-In Questionnaire.

10 Days After Move-In	"Warm and Fuzzy" phone call or personal stop at the apartment by Community Coordinator	Community Coordinator calls or stops by the apartment of the new resident to see if he or she needs anything or has any questions.
14 Days After Move-In	Maintenance Introduction	Maintenance confirms that resident understands how to use appliances in the apartment and reviews the maintenance request procedure.
30 Days After Move-In	Property Manager Contact	Property Manager sends a welcome letter to the resident.
60 Days After Move-In	Mail Satisfaction Questionnaire	Check the resident's satisfaction of community and home through a questionnaire.
90 Days After Move-In	"Warm and Fuzzy" Contact	Send a card to the resident from your team and have each staff member sign the card.

During Lease Term	Ongoing Contact	Send newsletters, flyers, and invites for events. Also, follow up on service requests for satisfaction concerns and conduct resident events.
180 Days After Move-In	"How Are We Doing" Questionnaire	Send out a short questionnaire for the resident to provide feedback.
During Lease Term	Ongoing Informal Contact	When staff meets the resident in the hallway, at an event, or at rent payment time, ask how things are in the apartment and if any service requests need to be written.
180 Days Prior To Lease Renewal	Resident Appreciation	Put a flower or seasonal gift on the doorstep of the resident's home with a note that says they are special. Have it signed by all the staff at the community.

120 Days Prior To Lease Renewal	Early Renewal	Send Letter to resident offering an "Early Renewal Bird Special" such as a small gift, carpet cleaning, or a lower increase on rent.
90 Days Prior To Lease Renewal	"We Want You to Stay" Card	Send a card signed by all staff.
60 Days Prior To Lease Renewal	"We Want You to Stay" Phone Call	Telephone call by the Community Coordinator to resident about the upcoming renewal.
45 Days Prior To Lease Renewal	Official Renewal Letter	Send renewal letter.
30 Days Prior To Lease Renewal	Renewal Preparations	Community Coordinator requests the resident make an appointment to sign the new lease.
14 Days Prior To Lease Renewal	Final Contact	Community Coordinator calls or visits the resident if he or she has not responded.

A Resident Retention Plan may seem like a daunting amount of work, but it results in less work in the long run because you can focus on keeping your current residents happy instead of spending so much time and energy on finding and screening new residents. Although the community manager usually has the ultimate responsibility for resident renewals and retention, it helps to divide the tasks among the different onsite team members. This will spread out the work and make the plan even more effective, because it becomes a team effort.

The Big Idea

Residents love being taken care of, and that does not just mean having maintenance done in their apartment. It means that the entire team—maintenance *and* the office—are taking care of them. Residents love it and stay longer because of it.

Solution 2:
Survey residents to find out what they like and dislike.

Surveys can now be easily done online for free as long as you have the residents' email addresses. If not, you can send out a paper survey to ask for suggestions or feedback. Keep surveys simple by asking no more than 5–10 multiple-choice questions. Do not ask open-ended, essay-style questions except for "Is there anything else you would like to share?"

Many professionals in the multi housing industry never check on residents to see if they are happy. Some residents have recommendations or concerns they never voice; they just move out. I used to assume that if a resident wanted to voice an opinion, then they would. But I did not realize that the residents who voiced their opinions without being asked were not the majority, so I was not addressing the concerns or needs of the majority. I had a suggestion box next to my office door, but the only things I found in there were used gum wrappers, never any slips of paper with ideas on them.

When I decided to ask for feedback, it was scary to ask people to tell me what they didn't like or what I was doing poorly. But it needed to be done if I was going to serve my residents and increase my retention rate. My first survey had 20 questions varying from maintenance performance to ideas for the summer resident event. I asked residents to drop off the surveys in the suggestion box as soon as possible, but I neglected to include a deadline. I didn't get one survey back. I felt like I had wasted my time, and it seemed obvious my residents didn't care.

But I thought, "There *must* be a way to get them to communicate with me about the community!" I did some research and decided to keep the surveys focused on one topic and shorten them to five questions with a multiple-choice rating system of 1–5. At the bottom, I had a section where residents could write any additional comment, concern, or recommendation not already covered. I also added a deadline with an incentive stating that completed surveys turned into the suggestion box by the deadline would be entered in a drawing for $50 off next month's rent.

These changes resulted in a wonderful response rate, with 40 out of 100 surveys returned to me.

I made a conscious effort to act on the survey responses

to show the residents that I valued their opinions and suggestions. If something came up that I could not do, I tried to come up with an alternative and let the residents know that I was attempting to work something out because I wanted them to be happy.

Send out Resident Satisfaction Surveys every quarter. Keep them short and related to a specific aspect of the community. For example, one survey might be about maintenance, and another about office hours. Always include an incentive for residents to complete the survey by a specific deadline, such as being entered in a drawing for $50 off next month's rent. You will discover what is important to and valued by current residents so you can make changes based on their recommendations and include them in the solution process. Residents become a loyal part of the team when they feel genuinely cared for.

SUGGESTED SURVEY TOPICS

- Residents' preferred type of communication (email, telephone, written notices, texting). *For a helpful guide on how to text residents from the company email address so staff does not need to give out their mobile numbers, see* **www.occupancysolutions.com/resources**.

- Maintenance performance related to residents' service requests.

- Why residents selected your apartment community to live in.

- Capital improvement ideas (provide a list of options you are considering).

- What services or social activities residents would like (provide options).

- What office hours best suit your residents (provide options).

- Annual resident event ideas (provide options).

The Big Idea

Asking your residents how you are doing or what improvements you need to make empowers you to know what your residents are thinking and how to keep or make them happy, which means they will become loyal to you and stay longer.

Solution 3
Host Townhall Meetings.

Hosting Townhall Meetings allows management to keep their residents informed and up to date on important information. These meetings allow residents to ask questions of the management team and gives the residents an opportunity to voice concerns and provide feedback to management.

TIPS FOR HOSTING A TOWNHALL MEETING

1. Keep the Opening Short. As the manager, you may feel the need to talk a lot! But you don't. Introduce the agenda so everyone knows what to expect, and then jump right in. It won't be fun for anyone if you drag things out longer than necessary.

2. Stick to the Agenda's Timing. Keep it simple. Explain time constraints to everyone and that you will keep to the agenda. Ensure that everyone sticks to their time limits. It doesn't say much for the management team if it promises a 90-minute meeting but goes on for three hours.

3. Celebrate Successes. Meetings provide an opportunity to celebrate the successes of your team, even small ones. It's great to use these meetings to drive your team harder, but that message is more likely to be well-received if you've already acknowledged the team's successes—especially if you acknowledge the team members in front of their peers.

4. Share Openly. Share information as openly and candidly as you can. It will help to build trust. While it would be imprudent to share certain sensitive information, share what you can.

5. Include Everyone. Invite all staff and residents to the meeting.

6. Discuss Key Metrics. All organizations have somewhere they're trying to get to. Share your metrics for important initiatives so everyone understands how the community is doing and what progress is being made.

7. Leave Room for Q & A. Leave time on the agenda for questions and answers. It's important to hear feedback from the residents and allow them to ask questions so they feel they understand everything. If you don't know the answer to a question, then say that you don't know and will get back to them. Don't try to make up an answer if you don't know it. You may feel like it makes you look better if you have an answer to everything, but it undermines your credibility if you lie.

8. Keep It Fun. Meetings can be a great opportunity to have some fun. This could be getting pizza or beer for everyone at the end of the meeting and encouraging them to socialize. Or it could be giving employees the opportunity to sing or dance to showcase their other talents. Use your imagination.

5

POOR MAINTENANCE

Solution 1:
Address maintenance problems
immediately and proactively.

Residents live in multifamily communities because they want to be taken care of and don't want to have to fix things. That is why they pay for maintenance. The worst situation is for residents to have maintenance issues in their apartments when it is time for renewal. When all they can think about is the fact that they have items that need attention in their home, it is very hard to convince them to renew.

Have the renewal meeting in the resident's apartment and, during the renewal discussion, have a maintenance technician there with tools in hand, ready to fix things right then so the residents are ready to renew immediately and feel that the customer service was excellent.

When we address problems immediately, residents see the value and feel like they are taken care of. Maintenance technicians at the meeting can do a preventative maintenance check and look for other minor issues the resident may have forgotten about or did not even notice.

If a resident has a problem in their apartment that requires a return visit or a vendor to address the problem, tell the resident what you will do, do it, and then make sure the resident knows you did it. Follow up and confirm that the resident knows the work was done.

This is the DuPont Theory:

1. Tell the resident what you will do.
2. Do it.
3. Tell the resident you did it.

I used to assume that residents would tell me if anything was wrong or needed fixing in their apartment. I would send out the renewal notices and be surprised when residents didn't respond. Or, if they did, they had a list of problems they wanted fixed before they signed their renewals. Some would not even tell me they had problems in their apartment. They would just move out because they felt they were not being taken care of.

I would send out my notices and start working the renewal system, leaving phone messages, handwritten notes under doors, emails, texts, and formal letters delivered by mail. I learned that residents who did not respond were often dragging their feet because they had a problem or a concern.

Mr. & Mrs. Johnston were a couple I called and called without getting a response. I started waiting near their apartment around the time they returned from work each day. One day, Mrs. Johnston returned home, and I met her in the walkway. I asked if she had a couple of minutes to discuss her lease which would be up in less than 30 days. She had her arms full of groceries, so I held the door for her and followed her into her home.

I suggested that maybe we could set up an appointment for her and her husband to come into the office to discuss their renewal. She was not very excited to see me. With a huge sigh, she agreed to discuss the renewal, but she was short on time, so I needed to do it right then while she put away her groceries. She reminded me that she and Mr. Johnston were incredibly busy people and didn't have time for a formal meeting any time soon.

While Mrs. Johnston put away her groceries, she complained that they had several maintenance items that needed attention, but they hadn't had the time to put in a service request or to wait for a maintenance technician to do the work, because they felt one of them needed to be there whenever anyone was in their home.

Right then, I radioed the maintenance supervisor, Tony. I asked him to stop by the office, pick up a blank service request (because I wanted to document everything properly) and grab his tools to do some basic, minor repairs in the Johnston's apartment. Within minutes, Tony arrived.

Mrs. Johnston was confused about why he was there. I explained to her that there was no time like the present to get working on the items in her home. She was there, and Tony was ready to work.

Tony took care of the items she identified during our walkthrough of the apartment. Tony also noticed the bathroom door was sticking, which Mrs. Johnston hadn't mentioned, so he fixed it. Tony also noticed a rattling whenever the central air came on. Mrs. Johnston hadn't mentioned that either, but Tony took care of it right then. Finally, Tony found something else she hadn't noticed: the screen door to her patio was off track. He fixed it immediately.

Mrs. Johnston was so appreciative! The whole appointment took less than 30 minutes, and she was ready, willing, and able to sign her lease right then.

Tony and I left her feeling great. It was a win/win/win. Mrs. Johnston was happy with her apartment, I got the lease signed, and Tony was a superhero.

Based on this experience, I thought, "Why wait for someone to complain? Why not do this all the time when maintenance is in the apartment anyway?" Now whenever we have an apartment inspection or when maintenance responds to a service request, maintenance takes basic tools and supplies so they can do more than just complete the service request. They are ready to make repairs on the spot even fix things the resident has not recognized as problems.

If maintenance has not been in a resident's apartment in several months because there have been no service requests, management and maintenance schedule a walkthrough about 30 days before the first renewal letter. Maintenance addresses items right then and there, so when the resident gets their renewal letter, they feel they have been well cared for, and that maintenance is taking a proactive approach to keeping their home in good working order.

The Big Idea

Do not wait for residents to complain. Engage maintenance technicians to address any problems residents have with their apartment—even things the residents haven't noticed yet. When fulfilling service requests, technicians should look for anything else that might need repaired and address it right away. Include technicians at the renewal meeting to take care of anything that is troubling the resident. Residents will be happier and more likely to renew.

Solution 2:
Do follow-up calls to make sure the residents are happy with the work done by maintenance and that the problem has been corrected.

One afternoon, I received a call from a very upset resident, Sonya, about her refrigerator. Apparently, she had put in a service request because her refrigerator was making a weird noise, and she said that maintenance never came to her apartment to fix it. I said I would check into it and call her right back.

My research showed that Sonya had put in a service request related to her refrigerator making a squeaking noise. Maintenance said they had taken of the problem, which was the circulating fan. They had replaced the rubber mounting grommets which showed signs of wear that would cause the noise, then they closed out the request. So why did Sonya feel the work was *not* done, when maintenance felt that they took care of the problem? And why was Sonya so upset?

It turns out that Sonya was upset because she felt like she was being ignored. She said the refrigerator was still squeaking and was driving her crazy.

I sent maintenance back to her apartment to fix the problem. This time, they said the refrigerator was working fine, and they left.

I got a call a few minutes later. Sonya was beside herself because the squeaking was back, so I sent maintenance again. Sonya was standing there with the refrigerator door open saying to maintenance as they walked in, "Can't you hear it? Can't you hear it?"

They could hear it, so they looked inside the refrigerator. The noise was not a maintenance issue at all. A Styrofoam egg container was rubbing against the inside of the refrigerator due to the vibrations, and it was the source of the squeaking.

After some laughs and a little embarrassment, Sonya apologized to all of us.

Two things went wrong in this situation. First, Sonya didn't know that maintenance had been in her apartment because there was no note, or anything left behind to tell her they had been there to fix the problem. The solution is to leave a copy of the service request or some indication that maintenance was there, what they determined to be the problem, and how they fixed it.

Second, no one in the office made a follow-up phone call to make sure that Sonya was happy with the work. The solution is to have a management representative follow up and confirm the resident feels the problem has been solved.

After this little fiasco, we implemented a new, three-step system.

1. After maintenance has done the work to satisfy the service request, the technician now leaves a copy of the service request noting the findings and the work performed in the apartment to correct the problem. They leave this copy on the kitchen counter for the resident to keep.

2. Before the completed service request is filed away, the office staff calls, texts, or emails the resident (based on the resident's preferred form of communication) to confirm the work was completed to the resident's satisfaction, and that the work area was left clean. This conversation is noted on the service request and, assuming there is a positive response, the request is filed away.

3. If the resident is not happy with the work because they feel it did not address the problem correctly or to the resident's satisfaction, this is noted on the service request and given back to maintenance to revisit. This cycle continues

until the resident is happy.

We also implemented a maintenance and service request log system so we could easily see which service requests are outstanding at any given time. (Many property management software solutions or web-based applications now include a system that tracks all service requests and their progress.) A service request is not marked "complete" until we receive confirmation from the resident. Then, we can confidently move on to the next service request, because we know the resident is happy and feels taken care of.

The Big Idea

Never assume the resident was happy with how a service request was fulfilled. Always follow up with a phone call, text, or email, and only close out the service request once the resident confirms they are completely happy with the work.

Solution 3:
Have maintenance leave a business card or a note stating who serviced the apartment; include a rating card encouraging the resident to complete and return the rating card and offer an incentive to get a higher response rate.

Our residents' apartments are their most personal space. They raise their children in these homes, store their most prized possessions within these rooms, and go to sleep every night feeling safe. When maintenance answers a service request, they are invading this very personal, private space, and it makes residents nervous. Residents wonder who was in the apartment, what they did, and how long they were in the apartment. Residents wonder, "Did people go through my things?"

How many times do our maintenance teams respond to a service request and leave only a copy of the service request, marked up and difficult to read—or nothing at all? Management assumes the resident was happy about the work, but never confirms it. When it is renewal time, the resident lists all the times a service request was not completed properly. And if he is paying for service, why should he renew?

I was negotiating a second-year renewal with Ms. Jones, who was a great resident. She paid her rent on time each month, she participated in community events, and she never had a lease violation. During our discussion, she brought up the fact that she had a service request for an outlet in her living room that did not work. Maintenance completed the service request, but Ms. Jones said that they didn't fix the outlet. She said that she just accepted it because she didn't want to be a bother or cause any problems. She also said that she was rather busy, and to call and try to explain the problem just seemed like a lot of work and time. She did receive a voicemail from my assistant asking about her satisfaction of the job, but Ms. Jones didn't have time and, she admitted, forgot to call back to explain her problem. But now that I was discussing her renewal, she was upset that the work in her apartment was never properly completed.

I wondered how my team could make communication easier for our busy residents. I sat down with my maintenance supervisor, Tony, and we brainstormed. We compared apartments to hotels. I had just stayed in a hotel on a recent vacation, so I thought about what they had done to make my stay better. The hotel had taken a couple important steps to make sure their guests were happy.

First, the hotel left a handwritten note that explained who had prepared the room for my stay. Great idea! We could leave handwritten notes for our residents, but Tony was concerned about how long it would take, and about the handwriting, spelling, and grammatical errors that might be included on those notes.

So, we agreed on creating a "maintenance business card" for his team that included the management office contact information, directions on the various ways to request service in the future, such as what email address to send requests to, instructions how to text the office a request for service, a telephone number to call in work requests, and how to complete a service request using the resident portal on our community website. On the other side of the card was a preprinted note: "It was a pleasure completing your service request." At the bottom of the card was a place for the technician completing the service request to write his name.

Plus, we created a brief rating card that we placed next to the completed service request and business card. On this card, we asked the resident to rate our service, including response time, cleanliness, and job completion satisfaction on a scale of one to five. We found that although maintenance was leaving this ratings card, very few residents completed them. So, we created a monthly drawing for a $50 gift card, and residents who completed the card would be entered in the drawing.

It worked wonderfully. With rating cards, we got feedback from residents about their experiences. For any rating cards that had a rating of three or less, we made sure to reach out to the resident to discuss their concerns, correct anything we needed to, and improve the resident's experience We learned and grew from the feedback. This helped us cater to the residents' needs and encouraged maintenance to get the best results.

The Big Idea

With a rating card, we can see how our team is doing and if residents are happy with the work performed in their apartment. Communication and feedback are the keys to providing exceptional customer service!

Solution 4:
Make sure a resident's apartment has no outstanding service requests when starting the renewal process.

43% of residents choose to rent because they want maintenance-free living. Residents should be happy about living at your community. If they are angry because they are waiting on an overdue repair, it is a bad time to ask them to stay longer. Complete all service requests before asking for another commitment. Timing is everything!

Often, we send out renewal notices without doing our due diligence first. Due diligence includes checking to see if residents have consistently paid rent on time, whether they have any unresolved concerns about their neighbors, whether their neighbors have any concerns about them, whether they are happy or unhappy with management, or if they have any pending service requests for their apartment. Unresolved problems in any of these areas signal that it is not a good time to send a renewal notice.

When I was a manager, I once sent out a batch of 20 renewal notices, including one to Mr. Murphy saying that his lease was coming to an end and it was time for him to renew. A couple of days later, my assistant manager said Mr. Murphy was on the phone asking to speak with me. I knew it had to be about his renewal notice, so I picked it up and said, "Hi, Mr. Murphy, how can I help you?"

Mr. Murphy started yelling at me and questioned at length my ability to manage the community. Once he took a breath, I cut in and asked him to please explain what exactly he was referring to. Apparently, Mr. Murphy had an ongoing problem in his apartment that my maintenance person was still working on. It was a small water leak near his bedroom window. Maintenance initially thought they had taken care of the problem by caulking the window, and everything was fine—until it rained again. Then the leak came back.

Each time maintenance looked at the leak, they thought it was fixed—until more rain came. After several months and numerous attempts to fix the leak, including having outside vendors look at it, the leak persisted. I had no idea it was still a problem, but I had sent out a renewal notice including a rent increase. This was why Mr. Murphy was so upset.

I put his renewal on hold while my team attempted to fix his leak. They finally found the leak in an area where the tuckpointing had failed. Once the leak was fixed, I sent Mr. Murphy another renewal notice, without an increase, and explained how sorry I was that he had experienced such a frustrating situation.

He renewed.

The Big Idea

If a resident is due for renewal but has a service request outstanding, address it before sending a renewal notice. Two weeks before sending the renewal letter, contact the resident to make sure everything is okay and ask if any work is needed. If so, take care of the service request ASAP. The resident will feel good and be more likely to sign the new lease.

6

CRIME

T HIS CHAPTER FOCUSES on reducing crime through activities that build and strengthen a sense of community. But, improving your resident selection criteria is also crucial to reducing crime. The first three solutions in Chapter 1 should be part of your overall crime-reduction strategy: increasing the minimum income requirement, raising the minimum credit score requirement, and performing landlord reference checks. You may not have as many people moving in, but you will have the *best* people moving in.

Solution 1:
Create a crime watch or neighborhood watch program that residents volunteer to participate in and work together to protect the community.

When residents are not part of the solution, they often ignore suspicious activity at the community, and in many cases do not know what to look for or how they can prevent criminal activity. Involving residents in solving the problem of crime includes encouraging them to take an active role in a community crime-prevention program.

Instituting a neighborhood watch program brings residents together to protect their homes and make the community safer for everyone. A great way to launch a neighborhood watch program is to have a group such as Crime Stoppers present at a resident meeting. This group can explain how residents can make a difference and share responsibility for protecting their community.

A neighborhood watch program should include a system for residents to report suspicious activity. Posting signs about the program will ensure that everyone who visits the community knows they are being watched by the neighbors.

The Big Idea

Involve residents in solving the problem of crime by creating a community program or neighborhood watch.

Solution 2:
Nurture a sense of community where residents get to know and recognize their neighbors.

In a true community, residents know their neighbors and will identify others as outsiders because they don't recognize strangers. If management does not nurture a sense of community, residents will come and go without knowing their neighbors. They will not be able to identify someone who should not be on the premises. Offering resident events creates an opportunity to encourage resident interaction and for the residents to meet others or at least become familiar with their neighbors. Without resident events or any support from management inspiring residents to get to know each other, crime tends to increase.

Create a plan to encourage residents to get to know each other and develop a sense of community. Include resident events and programs to introduce new residents to their neighbors. Engage residents to volunteer to be "floor captains" and act as a welcoming committee to introduce new residents to their neighbors. Use social media to connect neighbors, and host monthly events such as wine tastings, happy hours, and pizza parties.

The Big Idea

Nurture community by creating a plan that encourages residents to get to know and recognize each other.

7

NEGATIVE OR POOR COMMUNICATION

Solution 1:
Send thank-you notes, birthday cards, and anniversary (renewal) cards.

Sometimes, the only communication from management to residents is negative: nonpayment notices, lease violation notices, and notices informing residents of an inconvenient interruption of service. When we send positive communication, it softens the blow of some of the negative communication, and it shows our appreciation.

Send thank-you cards to residents who notify the management team of items needing repair or attention in the community, not just in their apartment. The residents are our eyes on the property, and we want to encourage them to take responsibility for the community. We can do this using the positive reinforcement of a thank-you card after a resident submits a service request for something in a common area or communal amenity.

Send birthday cards to all residents who have birthdays during the month; it will make them feel special by showing that we are thinking of them. Don't just send out a renewal letter; instead send a card to celebrate the resident's anniversary of moving into the community and becoming part of the family. The renewal information could be included in the card, but focus on their future with you, just like you would in any other relationship in which you celebrate an anniversary.

The Big Idea

Residents who experience positive correspondence will not dread hearing from management, and they will feel appreciated.

Solution 2:
Know how and when your residents like to communicate.

When we need to contact a resident, do we call, slip a note under their door, or mail a letter? Do we email them, or send a text message to their mobile phone? The answer should depend on the resident's stated preference.

Today, we might have up to five different generations living in one community, and different generations prefer to communicate differently. Technology offers a variety of ways for us to communicate. Ask for communication preferences early in the relationship, as early as when prospects first visit your community for a tour during their apartment search. Ask for their preferences about the best method and time of day to communicate. Track the answers on their guest card. Ask again for confirmation once a prospect moves in and becomes a resident, and also during their renewal.

Honor these preferences as much as possible. Residents

understand there will be some exceptions due to legal aspects or emergencies, but they will be grateful that you are making every attempt to respect them by communicating in their preferred way.

The Big Idea

Corresponding based on residents' preferences—not ours—provides exceptional customer service and makes for happier residents.

Solution 3:
Use language the resident can understand and relate to.

Different generations, cultures, and ethnic groups may use terminology or words that are different from those of the management and maintenance team. This can cause confusion and, in some cases, bad customer service.

In one community, a resident called in a service request about the "eye on her stove" not working properly. The office person wrote "eye on the stove not working" on the service request. The maintenance technician picked up the service request and went to the resident's apartment to fix the "eye on the stove". But when he got to the apartment, he read the service request again and realized he didn't know what "eye on the stove" meant. He returned to the office and asked the person who wrote up the service request, but she didn't know what it meant, either. They tried to contact the resident but couldn't reach her.

The resident returned home that evening, tired and exhausted from work, only to find the "eye on her stove" still didn't work. She contacted the office staff, who said that no one understood her request. She explained it was a burner.

The office staff now asks for clarification and more information when communicating with residents and other team members. Also, the staff is educated on the types of questions to ask and, in some cases, might even be able to help the resident fix a problem without a visit from a maintenance technician. For example, if the garbage disposal doesn't work, the staff will ask if the resident pushed the reset button. If the resident tries it and it works, then they don't need to wait for maintenance, and they know what to try first if it happens again.

Now, if a resident makes a service request about an "eye on her stove", the office person will write "eye on the stove not working" on the service request but also ask the resident to clarify what that means. If the resident explains it is a burner, the office staff includes "burner" on the service request so maintenance will understand and can fix it before the resident returns home that evening. Both employees will sufficiently understand the situation so they can provide excellent customer service.

It is also helpful to understand how best to communicate with the different generations at your community. To optimize your communication with someone, it is best to have some knowledge of how they like to be communicated with. We've all heard the advice, "Treat someone the way you would like to be treated," but I feel it is important to change our thinking and our actions to "Treat someone the way *they* want to be treated." Knowing which generation your resident belongs to will empower you to treat them better and communicate more successfully.

COMMUNICATION TECHNIQUES FOR DIFFERENT GENERATIONS

Silent Generation/Matures (1925–1942)
- Emphasize your experience.
- Find out what they want by asking questions.
- Communicate face-to-face.
- Offer discounts, focusing on savings and stress reduction.
- Highlight their active and independent lifestyle.

Baby Boomers (1943–1960)
- Body language is important.
- Answer questions thoroughly.
- Expect to be pressed for details.
- Present options.
- Provide highlights and summarize details so they can decide quickly.
- Show that you are resourceful.

Gen X (1961–1981)
- Use email or text as a primary communication tool.
- Talk in short sound bites to keep their attention.
- Ask them for their feedback and provide them with regular updates.
- Share information with them on a regular basis and keep them in the loop.
- Use an informal communication style.

Gen Y/Millennials/Echo Boomers (1982–1995)
- Use action words.
- Do not talk down to them. They will resent it.
- Use email or text communication.
- Seek their feedback constantly and provide them with regular updates.
- Use humor. Don't take yourself too seriously.

Gen Z (1986–early 2000s)
- Communicate in a timely manner through a platform of their choice.
- Be actively involved in all online conversations about the property.
- Offer an unmatched level of customer service and timely resolutions.
- Get all staff on board with training, policies, and resources.
- Incorporate online reputation management into the staff training programs.
- Have digital support specialists or a corporate communications team work together with onsite community staff.
- Respond to and acknowledge all reviews, whether positive or negative.
- Integrate testimonials into sales brochures.
- Be genuine. Don't remove existing comments or post fake reviews.
- Parents are important. Create a dedicated section on your website for resident testimonials and information for parents.

The Big Idea

Different people communicate differently. Tailor your communication style and platform to match your residents' preferences.

Solution 4:
Ask clarifying questions so you can communicate better with residents and other team members.

A resident reported her faucet was leaking. The office person wrote "faucet is leaking" on the service request. The maintenance technician picked up the request and went to the resident's apartment. He found the kitchen faucet was dripping, so he fixed it and turned in the completed service request to the office.

Several days later, another resident called because water was dripping from his bathroom ceiling. Maintenance rushed over to inspect the situation and discovered that the bathroom faucet in the apartment above was leaking. The upstairs resident told maintenance that she had called in a service request about her leaking faucet, but no one had taken care of the problem.

Apparently, the first resident did not call about her *kitchen* faucet but about her *bathroom* faucet, but no one asked enough questions to get the full picture. This resulted in increased repair costs and two very unhappy residents.

Now we train staff to ask more questions and to understand the situation better when communicating with residents and team members. If a resident says her faucet is leaking, the office staff knows to ask *which* faucet and what exactly the resident means by "leaking". This results in more detailed explanations to the maintenance technicians, such as, "The bathroom sink faucet is leaking underneath into the cabinet and does not stop when the faucet is turned off." Now maintenance knows how severe the problem is and exactly what needs repaired.

EXAMPLES OF QUESTIONS THAT CLARIFY THE PROBLEMS, LEAD TO BETTER COMMUNICATION WITH MAINTENANCE, AND PROVIDE EXCEPTIONAL CUSTOMER SERVICE:

- Does maintenance have permission to enter if the resident is not home?
- Which faucet is having problem? (The answer should include the room and which faucet; for example, guest bathroom bathtub.)
- Is the faucet dripping from above or below the counter?
- Is the faucet dripping continuously or only when the water is in use?
- Is it the hot-water or cold-water faucet?
- Did you try resetting the breaker?
- When did the problem start?
- When did you first notice the issue?
- Have you tried anything to fix it before calling us? If so, what?
- Did you try the lamp in another outlet to confirm that the lamp works properly, and that it is the outlet that is not working?

The Big Idea

Asking questions to create clarity means we are communicating well, which results in better customer service.

Solution 5:
Avoid using industry jargon when communicating with residents and prospects.

Using words that are resident-friendly reinforces a community feeling. They paint a warmer, communal picture that cold, harsh, industry jargon does not.

Are you using these "cold" words?
- Tenant
- Complex or Facility
- Unit or Room
- Work Order
- Waiting List
- Lease Expiration

Those words don't paint a warm, caring picture for residents.

Replace cold words with warm ones:
- Tenant = Resident or Neighbor
- Complex or Facility = Community or Neighborhood
- Unit or Room = Home, Apartment, Townhome, Loft ("Room" refers more to an assisted living or nursing home environment, but if you offer full apartments,

that's a big difference!)
- Work Order = Service Request
- Waiting List = Preferred Reservation List (No one wants to be on a list to wait!)
- Lease Expiration = Anniversary Date ("Lease expiration" sounds like it is time to move out!)

The Big Idea

Using customer-friendly words helps residents and prospects feel like they are at home and part of a community.

CONCLUSION

T HE ONSITE TEAM can enhance your residents' living experience by providing exceptional customer service and nurturing a sense of community. According to the National Apartment Association, feeling like a part of a community is an important factor when renters choose a building to call home.[1]

In fact, a sense of community is behind five of the top 10 apartment amenities that have been added or upgraded the most since 2014. These amenities include clubhouses and other common areas where residents can relax and socialize, as well as activity-focused spots, such as fitness and co-working spaces, that encourage like-minded residents to meet in the common areas of their buildings.

But a sense of community is about more than spaces for socializing; it involves making each resident feel like a part of something bigger. When I was a leasing consultant in the 1980s, we knew residents by their apartment numbers: "Mr. 208" and "Mrs. 544". By the late 90s, we realized that our residents preferred being called by their actual names!

Since then, we learned that knowing our residents' interests and hobbies also improves our relationships with them. Showing interest in our residents, noticing them and what they like to do, or recognizing when something is

---

[1] Munger, Paula. (2017). "Adding Value in the Age of Amenities". *National Apartment Association.* http://www.naahq.org/news-publications/units/may-2017/article/adding-value-age-amenities-wars

wrong and asking them about it, even striking up a simple conversation when we see them in the hall—all these actions enhance our residents' feeling of belonging to a community.

Ultimately, this community-based approach builds loyalty and increases resident retention.

ABOUT THE AUTHOR

E laine M. Simpson has worked in the housing industry since 1986. Starting onsite as a leasing agent, she moved up, working as assistant manager, site manager, executive director and finally senior regional manager with communities in several states and portfolios containing more than 1400 units. Elaine has extensive experience in Section 8, Section 236, and Low Income Housing Tax Credit programs, senior communities, and market rate and luxury apartment communities.

She has trained new managers across the country, assisted in creating Best Practices and procedure manuals, participated in numerous task forces during national mergers, acquisitions, and dispositions. Elaine has led turnaround teams assigned to troubled and distressed communities, successfully increasing income and reducing resident turnover while decreasing expenses and allowing the property to recover economic viability.

Elaine is a highly rated and sought-after national speaker, consultant, and trainer with offices in Detroit and Phoenix. She is known for going above and beyond to create workshops, trainings, and keynote presentations that are unique, engaging, and energizing. Sharing her stories about more than years in property management and corporate life, Elaine uses her relatable experiences, struggles, and successes to connect with anyone who has customers or employees. Using humor and interactive exercises, she grabs the audience and takes them for a ride they will enjoy and remember while learning important tools and concepts upon which success and results are built.

Elaine is the founder and president of Occupancy Solutions, LCC and has helped countless professionals with all of their leadership, operational, marketing, maintenance, human resources, housing compliance, leasing consulting, and training needs. She is a John Maxwell Certified Coach, Trainer, and Speaker, a member of the National Speaker Association, a faculty member of the National Apartment Association Education Institute and the International Board of Certified Trainers, a licensed real estate broker in Arizona and Michigan, and the Secretary of the Michigan Housing Council.

Elaine helps communities through proven, cost-effective techniques and strategies to achieve increased occupancy, improve resident retention, minimize expenses, and increase net operating income.

NOTES

NOTES

NOTES

NOTES

NOTES

NOTES

www.ingramcontent.com/pod-product-compliance
Lightning Source LLC
Chambersburg PA
CBHW052140270326
41930CB00012B/2964